pocket posh® brain games

100 PUZZLES

The Puzzle Society™
puzzlesociety.com

Andrews McMeel
Publishing, LLC
Kansas City · Sydney · London

ISBN-13: 978-0-7407-7989-3
ISBN-10: 0-7407-7989-3

All puzzles supplied under license from
Puzzler Media Ltd.—www.puzzler.com
www.andrewsmcmeel.com
www.PuzzleSociety.com

ATTENTION: SCHOOLS AND BUSINESSES
Andrews McMeel books are available at quantity discounts
with bulk purchase for educational, business, or sales
promotional use. For information, please write to: Special
Sales Department, Andrews McMeel Publishing, LLC,
1130 Walnut Street, Kansas City, Missouri 64106.

Totalized

Follow the instructions from top to bottom, starting with the number given to reach an answer at the foot of the ladder. Try to solve the problem in your head.

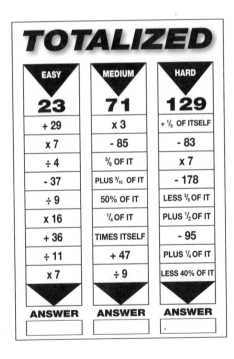

TOTALIZED

EASY	MEDIUM	HARD
23	**71**	**129**
+ 29	x 3	+ $\frac{1}{3}$ OF ITSELF
x 7	- 85	- 83
÷ 4	$\frac{5}{6}$ OF IT	x 7
- 37	PLUS $\frac{3}{10}$ OF IT	- 178
÷ 9	50% OF IT	LESS $\frac{3}{5}$ OF IT
x 16	$\frac{1}{4}$ OF IT	PLUS $\frac{1}{2}$ OF IT
+ 36	TIMES ITSELF	- 95
÷ 11	+ 47	PLUS $\frac{1}{4}$ OF IT
x 7	÷ 9	LESS 40% OF IT
ANSWER	**ANSWER**	**ANSWER**

Jigsaw

Use the jigsaw pieces to re-create this completed crossword. Only the clues for the Across words have been given, but the pattern of the grid should help you as it is symmetrical from top right to bottom left.

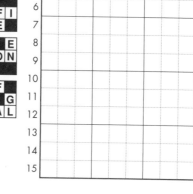

ACROSS

1 Import duty
2 Be in debt
3 Word for word, exact (translation)
4 Every part (of)
5 Evil spirit
6 Take part in a winter sport
7 Show a response
8 West Country high point • Electrically charged particle
9 Consumed
10 Adhesive substance
11 Pummel (dough)
12 Limb
13 Bringing up, raising
14 Make mistakes
15 Arranged (hair) in a particular way

Futoshiki

Fill the blank squares so that each row and column contains all the numbers 1, 2, and 3. Use the given numbers and the symbols to indicate if the number in the square is larger (>) or smaller (<) than the number next to it.

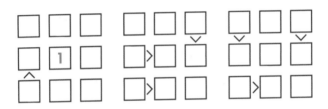

Fitword

Place all but one of the listed words in the grid. When the grid is complete, which word is left over?

3 letters	5 letters	6 letters
Ace	Charm	Martyr
Ago	Giver	Moaner
Asp	Imago	
Col	Livid	
Ilk	Motto	
Ill	Nears	
Kin		
Lie		
Wit		

4 letters
~~Fell~~
Fowl
Fume
Glut
Goal
Idly
Once
Rump
Slum

Number Jig

Place all but one of the listed numbers in the grid. When the grid is complete, which number is left over?

3 digits		
132	9012	49035
179	9214	53295
~~357~~	9849	57409
555		
833	5 digits	7 digits
859	35977	5654565
	39972	5676765
4 digits	41453	
1805		
2861		
3054		
3450		
3489		
3844		
4509		
4510		
6602		
7553		
7768		
7786		
8624		
8868		

4

Pathfinder

Beginning with TURMERIC, and moving up, down, left, or right, one letter at a time, trace a path of eighteen herbs and spices in the grid.

M	E	S	O	G	L	E	E	F	K	E
A	I	L	R	I	N	N	G	R	E
R	S	Y	E	L	G	E	R	U	F	T
Y	A	B	R	S	A	R	M	N	E	N
D	I	L	A	P	M	O	A	E	M	I
C	A	L	C	U	T	J	R	M	T	R
I	K	I	A	R	M	E	R	Y	H	E
N	N	R	R	D	E	G	I	C	O	D
M	A	P	A	A	M	A	N	A	R	N
O	A	R	P	M	O	S	O	G	E	A
N	T	R	A	G	O	N	C	O	R	I

Set Square

Place one each of the digits 1–9 in each grid to make the sums work. Sums should be solved from left to right, or from top to bottom.

	+	7	−		= 3
+		−		−	
9	+		÷		= 2
−		×		×	
	+		+		= 11

= 11   = 18   = 18

	×		+		= 19
+		×		×	
1	+		−		= 6
×		÷		−	
	×	6	−		= 23

= 15   = 12   = 5

2

Mini Jigsaw

Fit the pieces in the grid to spell a container in each row.

1		A				
2						
3						
4					A	
5						A
6						

S	K
T	B

A	R
E	T

C	A
H	A

M	O
P	U

B	U
S	H

R	T
N	N

E	T
O	X

E	T
T	H

C	K
E	A

Pathfinder

Beginning with FOOD PROCESSOR, and moving up, down, left, or right, one letter at a time, trace a path of fifteen items you might find in a kitchen.

F	O	O	C	P	R	E	N	D	W	H
R	P	D	I	L	S	S	A	E	R	I
O	S	S	A	R	C	O	L	E	C	S
C	E	O	G	L	N	A	C	P	U	K
L	L	R	O	W	O	P	N	A	A	S
E	A	M	B	G	N	E	L	E	N	D
T	N	M	I	N	E	R	B	I	Y	E
S	I	T	X	I	D	A	G	N	R	R
P	A	E	C	E	L	L	P	R	F	S
U	T	K	A	R	M	N	A	E	E	I
L	A	T	H	E	O	M	E	T	V	E

Number Jig

Place all but one of the listed numbers in the grid. When the grid is complete, which number is left over?

3 digits	8760	46002
150	8924	61029
376	9480	65739
456		
459	5 digits	7 digits
~~470~~	23456	5758595
479	33456	5958575
	45050	

4 digits
1525
3456
3595
4162
4175
4184
4892
6269
6479
6540
6830
7294
7654
8620

Fitword

Place all but one of the listed words in the grid. When the grid is complete, which word is left over?

3 letters
Air
Awe
Eau
Few
Fin
Ply
Sip
Sow
Sup
~~Web~~

4 letters
Able
Ante
Grab
Lobe
Loft
Skim
Snub
Stab

5 letters
Bingo
Blink
Haste
Leant
Upset
Whizz

6 letters
Asthma
Enzyme

Futoshiki

Fill the blank squares so that each row and column contains all the numbers 1, 2, and 3. Use the given numbers and the symbols to indicate if the number in the square is larger (>) or smaller (<) than the number next to it.

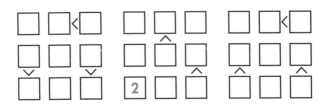

Set Square

Place one each of the digits 1–9 in each grid to make the sums work. Sums should be solved from left to right, or from top to bottom.

	+	9	−		= 7
×		+		×	
7	+		÷		= 2
−		−		÷	
	+		÷		= 7

= 15   = 2   = 10

	×		÷	3	= 16
×		÷		×	
	+		×	2	= 10
−		−		+	
	+		−		= 11

= 15   = 1   = 11

Mini Jigsaw

Fit the pieces in the grid to spell an agricultural term in each row.

1			
2			L
3	S L	U R	R Y
4	M A	N U	R E
5			
6		L	

D D	L L	R Y
T T	L A	R E

O W	F A	U R
G E	S I	N U

S L	E R	F O
M A	L E	C A

Cell Block

Complete the grid by drawing blocks along the grid lines. Each block must contain the number of squares indicated by the digit inside it. Each block must contain only one digit and be a rectangle or square.

4				3	
					3
			6		
	6	4			2
		1			
3				4	

Initials

If **ITHOTN** (Oscar-winning film) is *In the Heat of the Night,* what do these initials represent?

1 **SAD** (Biblical lovers)

_____

2 **ROTLA** (Harrison Ford film)

_____

3 **TKAM** (Classic novel and film)

_____

4 **TGGB** (National landmark)

_____

5 **PAP** (Classic novel)

_____

Jigsaw

Use the jigsaw pieces to re-create this completed crossword. Only the clues for the Across words have been given, but the pattern of the grid should help you as it is symmetrical from top right to bottom left.

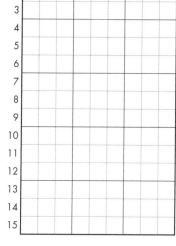

ACROSS

1 Portable lights
2 African wildebeest
3 Of some fame
4 Hardskinned fleshy fruit
5 Open
6 Sling, hurl
7 Disburden

9 Retainer
10 Fill with deilight
11 Let down
12 Ventilated
13 Take on as your own

14 Noah's boat
15 Principal bullfighter

Totalized

Follow the instructions from top to bottom, starting with the number given to reach an answer at the foot of the ladder. Try to solve the problem in your head.

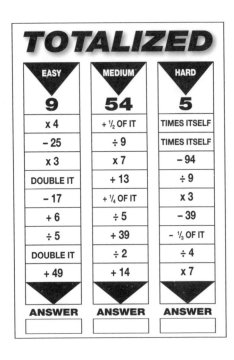

TOTALIZED

EASY	MEDIUM	HARD
9	**54**	**5**
x 4	+ ½ OF IT	TIMES ITSELF
− 25	÷ 9	TIMES ITSELF
x 3	x 7	− 94
DOUBLE IT	+ 13	÷ 9
− 17	+ ¼ OF IT	x 3
+ 6	÷ 5	− 39
÷ 5	+ 39	− ⅓ OF IT
DOUBLE IT	÷ 2	÷ 4
+ 49	+ 14	x 7
▼	▼	▼
ANSWER	**ANSWER**	**ANSWER**

Initials

If **ITHOTN** (Oscar-winning film) is *In the Heat of the Night*, what do these initials represent?

1 **HDD** (Nursery rhyme)

_____

2 **TWOTW** (H. G. Wells novel)

_____

3 **POTC** (Johnny Depp film)

_____

4 **GBR** (Australian coastal feature)

_____

5 **OGTDA** (Proverb)

_____

Cell Block

Complete the grid by drawing blocks along the grid lines. Each block must contain the number of squares indicated by the digit inside it. Each block must contain only one digit and be a rectangle or square.

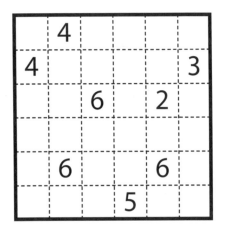

Mini Jigsaw

Fit the pieces in the grid to spell a sewing term in each row.

1			**N**
2			
3		**N**	
4			
5	**N**		
6			

N G	L I	C O
I C	F A	T H

E D	N E	N I
I T	S T	B R

T T	L E	O N
R E	C H	A D

Set Square

Place one each of the digits 1–9 in each grid to make the sums work. Sums should be solved from left to right, or from top to bottom.

3	×		+		= 20
×		+		×	
	+	4	−		= 10
−		÷		+	
	+		−		= 6

=		=		=
12		2		10

	+	8	÷		= 3
×		+		+	
	+		−	3	= 2
−		+		+	
	+		−		= 13

=		=		=
19		15		10

Pathfinder

Beginning with HANSEL, and moving, up, down, left, or right, one letter at a time, trace a path of thirteen fairytale and nursery rhyme characters.

E	R	G	A	N	I	M	U	G	R	E
T	E	M	B	E	L	P	H	O	O	H
P	L	U	H	T	Y	T	L	E	S	T
E	W	W	T	E	D	S	E	U	M	O
T	O	H	I	M	U	N	T	H	B	M
E	N	S	S	P	H	A	M	S	U	P
R	P	I	G	T	Y	T	O	S	I	S
N	A	P	E	L	T	S	T	B	N	K
R	A	P	T	T	H	R	O	O	O	C
Z	N	U	I	L	E	E	N	G	L	I
E	L	A	L	A	D	D	I	O	L	D

Number Jig

Place all but one of the listed numbers in the grid. When the grid is complete, which number is left over?

3 digits	7958	59674
354	9244	72679
364	9671	74754
367		
527	5 digits	7 digits
~~564~~	33455	7453621
567	35482	7653421
	57859	

4 digits
2215
2573
3274
5178
5241
5624
5629
5678
5726
6743
7139
7459
7477
7677

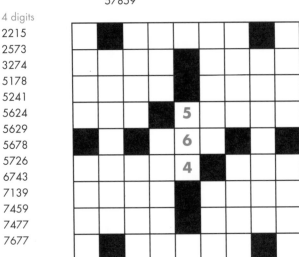

Fitword

Place all but one of the listed words in the grid. When the grid is complete, which word is left over?

3 letters	5 letters	6 letters
~~Bed~~	Bulky	Assure
Bib	Early	Rhymes
Bog	Icing	
Den	Khaki	
Ebb	Sulky	
Eye	Unity	
One		
Rig		
Spa		

4 letters
Aged
Byte
Dyed
Edgy
Holy
Make
Musk
Swig
Tsar

Futoshiki

Fill the blank squares so that each row and column contains all the numbers 1, 2, and 3. Use the given numbers and the symbols to indicate if the number in the square is larger (>) or smaller (<) than the number next to it.

Jigsaw

Use the jigsaw pieces to re-create this completed crossword. Only the clues for the Across words have been given, but the pattern of the grid should help you as it is symmetrical from top right to bottom left.

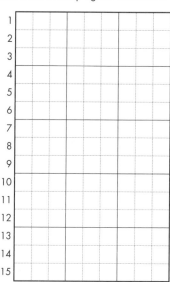

ACROSS

1 Tawdry, dirty
3 High title of sovereignty
4 Deciduous tree
5 Accuse of a serious crime
6 Roll or knot of hair
7 Set upon, attack
8 Sound-sensitive organ • Pinch
9 Great multitude
10 Large rounded vase
11 Sorrowful
12 Nervous mannerism
13 Obscure
15 Hindu place of worship

Totalized

Follow the instructions from top to bottom, starting with the number given to reach an answer at the foot of the ladder. Try to solve the problem in your head.

TOTALIZED

EASY	MEDIUM	HARD
9	**48**	**13**
x 5	÷ 12	TIMES ITSELF
+ 11	TIMES ITSELF	+ 76
÷ 8	x 11	÷ 5
+ 24	÷ 4	x 7
x 3	+ 27	− 196
− 51	x 3	÷ 3
÷ 3	+ 39	+ 23
+ 18	− 72	⁵⁄₆ OF IT
DOUBLE IT	÷ 9	+ ³⁄₅ OF IT
ANSWER	**ANSWER**	**ANSWER**

Initials

If **ITHOTN** (Oscar-winning film) is *In the Heat of the Night*, what do these initials represent?

1   **DTH** (Christmas carol)

_____

2   **MFL** (Musical)

_____

3   **GWTW** (Movie)

_____

4   **TBOTRK** (Prisoner-of-war film)

_____

5   **TJF** (Family group)

_____

Cell Block

Complete the grid by drawing blocks along the grid lines. Each
block must contain the number of squares indicated by the digit
inside it. Each block must contain only one digit and be a rectangle
or square.

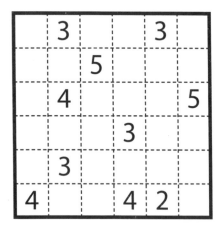

Mini Jigsaw

Fit the pieces in the grid to spell a printing term in each row.

1				**M**	
2					
3	**M**				
4					
5			**M**		
6					

F O	A T	M N
O F	E T	T A

M A	R G	C O
L E	T T	E R

I N	L U	R M
E R	R A	F S

Set Square

Place one each of the digits 1–9 in each grid to make the sums work. Sums should be solved from left to right, or from top to bottom.

	×		−		= 7
×		×		+	
	−	6	+		= 10
−		÷		−	
5	+		−		= 10

=
9

=
3

=
7

	÷	3	+		= 11
+		×		−	
	+		−	7	= 5
÷		−		+	
	÷		×		= 10

=
7

=
11

=
7

Pathfinder

Beginning with BREATHING, and moving up, down, left, or right, one letter at a time, trace a path of seventeen words concerning yoga classes.

U	T	I	N	E	S	T	A	M	O	P
O	R	E	V	U	T	R	T	E	S	D
M	P	R	O	R	C	U	S	T	I	L
I	Y	R	C	E	C	T	E	R	H	C
I	T	A	N	I	H	I	O	N	V	E
L	T	A	E	N	G	T	B	P	I	T
I	H	H	T	I	H	A	R	O	S	I
B	A	C	I	B	A	T	E	S	O	P
I	C	S	O	A	M	I	A	E	S	X
X	O	N	U	G	E	D	T	H	R	A
E	L	F	S	O	Y	G	N	I	E	L

Number Jig

Place all but one of the listed numbers in the grid. When the grid is complete, which number is left over?

3 digits
212
240
313
318
~~453~~
459

4 digits
1154
1740
2532
2552
2800
2802
3408
3611
4371
4614
4656
4666
5160
5341
5348
5481
9600

5 digits
23434
25163
35162
36152
43434
56153

7 digits
4445666
4455566

Fitword

Place all but one of the listed words in the grid. When the grid is complete, which word is left over?

3 letters
Ado
Aft
And
Due
Dye
Oil
Pet
Thy
Use

4 letters
Days
Flog
Fond
Gosh
Mine
Mire
Myth
~~Pyre~~
Tsar

5 letters
Flown
Heady
Kitty
Natty
Nylon
Sooty

6 letters
Ranked
Smoked

PYRE

35

Futoshiki

Fill the blank squares so that each row and column contains all the numbers 1, 2, and 3. Use the given numbers and the symbols to indicate if the number in the square is larger (>) or smaller (<) than the number next to it.

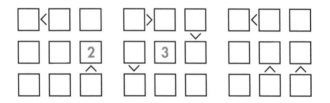

Jigsaw

Use the jigsaw pieces to re-create this completed crossword. Only the clues for the Across words have been given, but the pattern of the grid should help you as it is symmetrical from top right to bottom left.

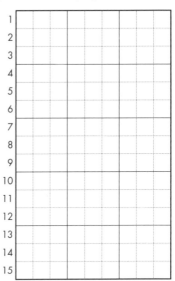

ACROSS

1 _____ bag
2 Mineral-bearing material
3 Scorch
4 Hanging loosely
5 Of the countryside
6 Select group
7 Sound a horn
8 Small horse-like animal
9 Title of Russian emperors
10 Porcupine's spine
11 Provide
12 Punctuation mark signifying a pause
13 Female family member
14 Runner for snow
15 Reserved, self-effacing

37

Totalized

Follow the instructions from top to bottom, starting with the number given to reach an answer at the foot of the ladder. Try to solve the problem in your head.

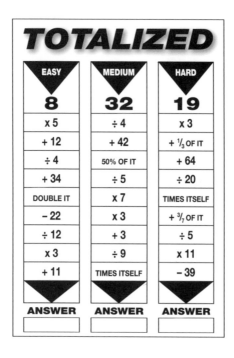

TOTALIZED

EASY	MEDIUM	HARD
8	**32**	**19**
x 5	÷ 4	x 3
+ 12	+ 42	+ 1/3 OF IT
÷ 4	50% OF IT	+ 64
+ 34	÷ 5	÷ 20
DOUBLE IT	x 7	TIMES ITSELF
− 22	x 3	+ 3/7 OF IT
÷ 12	+ 3	÷ 5
x 3	÷ 9	x 11
+ 11	TIMES ITSELF	− 39
ANSWER	ANSWER	ANSWER

Initials

If **ITHOTN** (Oscar-winning film) is *In the Heat of the Night*, what do these initials represent?

1 **TBOH** (1066 event)

_____

2 **THGOB** (Wonder of the world)

_____

3 **ML** (Famous portrait)

_____

4 **SBFSB** (Musical)

_____

5 **HP** (Fictional detective)

_____

Cell Block

Complete the grid by drawing blocks along the grid lines. Each block must contain the number of squares indicated by the digit inside it. Each block must contain only one digit and be a rectangle or square.

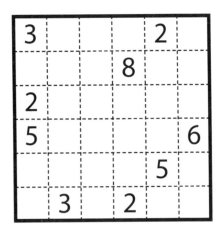

Mini Jigsaw

Fit the pieces in the grid to spell a cuisine or cookery term in each row.

1	R		
2			
3		R	
4			
5			R
6			

C O	R E	U R
R A	P I	T I

M M	P E	C I
F F	I C	C N

S E	S I	E R
O N	B U	E T

Set Square

Place one each of the digits 1–9 in each grid to make the sums
work. Sums should be solved from left to right, or from top to bottom.

	×	6	÷		= 15
+		×		×	
9	+		−		= 2
−		×		÷	
	−		×		= 16

=	=	=
7	18	4

	×		+	4	= 10
×		×		+	
	×	6	−		= 23
−		÷		÷	
	+		−		= 16

=	=	=
2	2	11

Pathfinder

Beginning with CENTIPEDE, and moving up, down, left, or right, one letter at a time, trace a path of eighteen creepy-crawlers.

M	P	R	G	C	R	I	E	T	E	R
R	Y	A	U	L	S	C	K	B	T	F
O	I	N	G	M	E	D	E	U	T	L
W	S	S	I	A	I	L	P	F	L	Y
U	G	L	T	N	M	L	I	E	E	W
B	C	O	C	U	L	I	D	G	A	A
Y	E	N	T	S	E	V	I	M	P	S
D	A	T	S	P	E	W	L	I	A	N
A	L	I	P	I	D	E	R	F	R	S
D	I	C	E	D	E	G	R	I	U	Y
A	C	Y	L	F	N	E	E	T	F	L

Number Jig

Place all but one of the listed numbers in the grid. When the grid is complete, which number is left over?

3 digits	6819	44079
318	6828	76672
360	9186	97408
374		
408	5 digits	7 digits
~~412~~	36628	1852647
859	37668	5264781
	42207	

4 digits
2088
2482
2828
3265
3478
3482
4150
4259
4529
5172
5428
6150
6710
6715

Fitword

Place all but one of the listed words in the grid. When the grid is complete, which word is left over?

3 letters	5 letters	6 letters
All	Array	Dahlia
Coo	Laced	Dulcet
Ego	Money	
Let	Panel	
Odd	Troll	
Opt	Uncut	
Rid		
Tat		
Tot		

4 letters
Abut
Amid
Arty
Eden
~~Hymn~~
Racy
Rate
Riot
Type

H Y M N

Futoshiki

Fill the blank squares so that each row and column contains all the numbers 1, 2, and 3. Use the given numbers and the symbols to indicate if the number in the square is larger (>) or smaller (<) than the number next to it.

Jigsaw

Use the jigsaw pieces to re-create this completed crossword. Only the clues for the Across words have been given, but the pattern of the grid should help you as it is symmetrical from top right to bottom left.

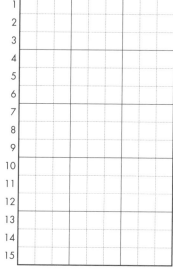

ACROSS

2 Indistinct shape •
  Measure of time
3 The "I"
4 Speed • Step of
  a ladder
5 Bygone
6 Charged particle
  • Achieved
7 Female gander

8 Boat race team •
  Operatic song
9 Spills liquid
10 Pan • Rage
11 Flowed back
12 Vein of metal ore •

Gave temporarily
13 Frozen water
14 Eagerly expectant
  • Maize

47

Totalized

Follow the instructions from top to bottom, starting with the number given to reach an answer at the foot of the ladder. Try to solve the problem in your head.

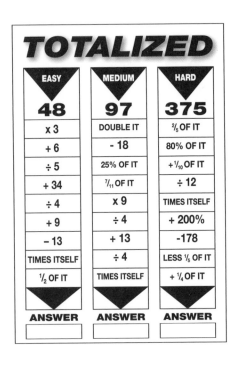

TOTALIZED

EASY	MEDIUM	HARD
48	**97**	**375**
x 3	DOUBLE IT	²/₅ OF IT
+ 6	– 18	80% OF IT
÷ 5	25% OF IT	+ ¹/₁₀ OF IT
+ 34	⁷/₁₁ OF IT	÷ 12
÷ 4	x 9	TIMES ITSELF
+ 9	÷ 4	+ 200%
– 13	+ 13	-178
TIMES ITSELF	÷ 4	LESS ¹/₅ OF IT
½ OF IT	TIMES ITSELF	+ ¼ OF IT
ANSWER	**ANSWER**	**ANSWER**

Initials

If **ITHOTN** (Oscar-winning film) is *In the Heat of the Night*, what do these initials represent?

1 **AWPNB** (Proverb)

_____

2 **SB** (Classic Italian dish)

_____

3 **TOATP** (Edward Lear children's poem)

_____

4 **TWOE** (Jack Nicholson film)

_____

5 **MHWGO** (No. 1 hit and film theme)

_____

Cell Block

Complete the grid by drawing blocks along the grid lines. Each block must contain the number of squares indicated by the digit inside it. Each block must contain only one digit and be a rectangle or square.

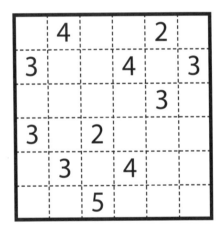

Mini Jigsaw

Fit the pieces in the grid to spell a chemical element in each row.

1	**R**		
2			
3		**R**	
4			
5			**R**
6			

U M	R B	L V
E L	P P	L I

S I	E R	D I
H E	U M	C K

C A	R A	O N
C O	N I	E R

Set Square

Place one each of the digits 1–9 in each grid to make the sums work. Sums should be solved from left to right, or from top to bottom.

9	−		×		= 21
+		+		+	
	+		−		= 5
−		÷		−	
	+	4	÷		= 1

=   =   =
15   2   6

6	÷		+		= 11
−		×		+	
	×		−	7	= 20
×		−		−	
	×		+		= 21

=   =   =
15   14   14

52

Pathfinder

Beginning with WHITE, and moving up, down, left, or right, one letter at a time, trace a path of eighteen colors.

V	A	O	S	W	H	I	H	A	L	P
E	L	N	M	T	N	T	E	Z	E	U
N	C	R	I	A	E	M	E	N	I	R
D	E	U	L	B	G	A	R	A	R	P
E	R	I	O	I	N	E	T	M	A	L
M	A	L	N	R	A	U	L	U	R	E
B	E	I	O	C	M	A	U	S	H	A
T	R	M	R	H	D	A	Q	S	K	K
U	E	V	E	R	L	O	G	E	T	I
R	S	I	S	E	L	E	N	D	I	V
Q	U	O	C	A	R	T	A	I	R	I

Number Jig

Place all of the listed numbers in the grid. There's no starter number placed in the grid but begin with the seven-digit numbers.

3 digits	5 digits	77127
200	13004	93063
250	16309	
262	23528	7 digits
506	24607	8283848
560	63520	8283849
654	69703	
674		
953		

4 digits
1508
1622
2048
2968
3420
3423
7318
7645
8318
8536
8705
9094

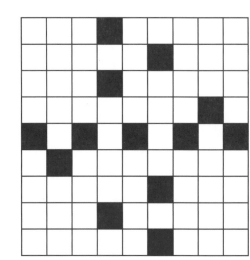

Fitword

Place all but one of the listed words in the grid. When the grid is complete, which word is left over?

3 letters	5 letters	6 letters
Ago	Aback	Parted
Are	Awful	Phoned
Fax	Lower	
Fen	Newer	
Gap	Nifty	
Gym	Spoof	
Off		
One		
Tog		
Who		

4 letters
Cowl
Cusp
Dole
Hemp
Hoax
Skep
Slip
~~True~~

Futoshiki

Fill the blank squares so that each row and column contains all the numbers 1, 2, and 3. Use the given numbers and the symbols to indicate if the number in the square is larger (>) or smaller (<) than the number next to it.

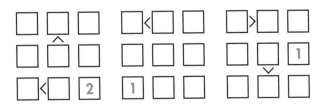

Jigsaw

Use the jigsaw pieces to re-create this completed crossword. Only the clues for the Across words have been given, but the pattern of the grid should help you as it is symmetrical from top right to bottom left.

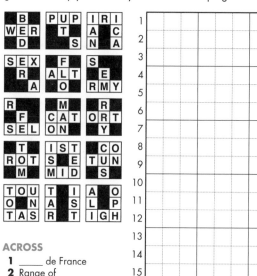

ACROSS

1 _____ de France
2 Range of saxophone
3 Tuft of threads
4 Chrysalis
5 Ship's left side
6 Exhale audibly
7 Camp bed
8 Canned food fish • Style of jazz singing
9 Weight of 2,000 pounds
10 Part of the eye
11 Schedule
12 Land-based military force
13 Biased on the grounds of gender
14 Wide-mouthed jug
15 Surrounded by

Totalized

Follow the instructions from top to bottom, starting with the number given to reach an answer at the foot of the ladder. Try to solve the problem in your head.

TOTALIZED

EASY	MEDIUM	HARD
13	**17**	**19**
+ 41	x 3	TIMES ITSELF
÷ 6	– 27	– 74
x 3	x 6	÷ 7
– 12	÷ 12	TRIPLE IT
x 4	x 8	+ ⅔ OF IT
– 12	+ 14	+ ⅗ OF IT
÷ 8	÷ 10	÷ 4
x 4	TIMES ITSELF	+ 83
+ 19	– 54	⅗ OF IT

ANSWER	ANSWER	ANSWER

Initials

If **ITHOTN** (Oscar-winning film) is *In the Heat of the Night*, what do these initials represent?

1 **PM** (Fruity dessert)

_____

2 **BCATSK** (Western)

_____

3 **AS** (Autumn vegetable)

_____

4 **SC** (Part of the Vatican)

_____

5 **VVG** (Dutch artist)

_____

Cell Block

Complete the grid by drawing blocks along the grid lines. Each
block must contain the number of squares indicated by the digit
inside it. Each block must contain only one digit and be a rectangle
or square.

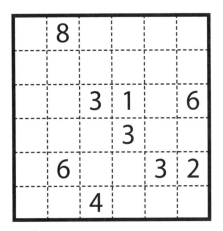

Mini Jigsaw

Fit the pieces in the grid to spell a type of bird in each row.

```
1 [  |  |  |  |  ]
2 [O |  |  |  |  ]
3 [  |  |  |  |  ]
4 [  |  |O |  |  ]
5 [  |  |  |  |O ]
6 [  |  |  |  |  ]
```

| S E | G R | G A |
| L E | O R | O S |

| C K | O U | O O |
| O V | I O | E R |

| N N | E T | C U |
| P R | E Y | P L |

Set Square

Place one each of the digits 1–9 in each grid to make the sums
work. Sums should be solved from left to right, or from top to bottom.

	−	3	×		= 12
+		×		×	
1	×		+		= 10
÷		−		−	
	+		−		= 4

=   =   =
2   5   4

	+		−	5	= 10
−		×		+	
	−	4	+		= 4
×		÷		÷	
	×		÷		= 12

=   =   =
6   3   3

Pathfinder

Beginning with JUDGES, and moving up, down, left, or right, one letter at a time, trace a path of seventeen Old Testament books.

```
E  D  L  E  C  I  T  I  V  H  A
U  E  K  I  U  O  N  A  E  L  I
T  Z  E  B  S  J  J  H  R  E  M
E  R  J  O  A  H  O  S  E  J  H
N  O  L  A  B  A  U  H  M  I  A
O  I  E  K  K  J  G  E  S  C  I
M  N  E  K  U  U  D  M  E  A  D
Y  A  X  O  A  H  L  A  N  H  A
N  D  H  D  I  N  A  H  T  O  B
A  H  A  U  S  Z  E  P  A  T  I
M  U  I  M  E  H  E  N  S  N  O
```

Number Jig

Place all of the listed numbers in the grid. There's no starter number placed in the grid but begin with the seven-digit numbers.

3 digits
342
345
462
541
545
664
727
800

4 digits
2024
2204
4271
4528
4581
5735
5738
6115
6176
6716
8714
8735

5 digits
55431
57231
67032
67236
67436
74131
75082
75251

7 digits
1345678
2345678

Fitword

Place all but one of the listed words in the grid. When the grid is complete, which word is left over?

3 letters
Apt
Bay
Bin
Imp
Pin
Rib
Rig
Sty
Tat

4 letters
Adze
Aged
Dupe
Dyer
Eyed
Game
Open
Pair
Rote

5 letters
Aired
~~April~~
Array
Ennui
Erect
Inert

6 letters
Holier
Relief

Futoshiki

Fill the blank squares so that each row and column contains all the numbers 1, 2, and 3. Use the given numbers and the symbols to indicate if the number in the square is larger (>) or smaller (<) than the number next to it.

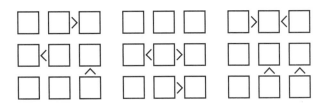

Jigsaw

Use the jigsaw pieces to re-create this completed crossword. Only the clues for the Across words have been given, but the pattern of the grid should help you as it is symmetrical from top right to bottom left.

ACROSS

1 Bespatter •
   Soup dish
2 Poem specifically
   addressed
3 Tree limb
4 Before now •
   Frozen hazard
5 Bottomless hole
6 Cat's sound •
   Operator
7 Badly, wrongly

8 Racing probability
   • Hollow pipe
9 Hot beverage
10 Ring of bells •
   Knob, lump
11 Go over again

12 Edge, border •
   Geological period
13 Feel longing (for)
14 Never mind which
15 Try to lose weight •
   Eastern ruler

Totalized

Follow the instructions from top to bottom, starting with the number given to reach an answer at the foot of the ladder. Try to solve the problem in your head.

TOTALIZED

EASY	MEDIUM	HARD
27	**156**	**456**
+ 53	75% OF IT	⁵/₆ OF IT
DOUBLE IT	+ 18	- 93
÷ 5	³/₅ OF IT	³/₇ OF IT
- 13	⁷/₉ OF IT	+ 381
DOUBLE IT	¹/₃ OF IT	x 3
+ 19	x 6	66⅔% OF IT
– 13	- 38	- 7
x 11	25% OF IT	÷ 11
¹/₄ OF IT	x 7	÷ 13
▼	▼	▼
ANSWER	**ANSWER**	**ANSWER**

Initials

If **ITHOTN** (Oscar-winning film) is *In the Heat of the Night*, what do these initials represent?

1 **KK** (Film monster)

_____

2 **DAG** (Biblical enemies)

_____

3 **TLTOP** (World landmark)

_____

4 **FAMD** (Animal illness)

_____

5 **SAG** (Singing duo)

_____

Cell Block

Complete the grid by drawing blocks along the grid lines. Each block must contain the number of squares indicated by the digit inside it. Each block must contain only one digit and be a rectangle or square.

1		5			
	4		2	2	
				2	2
6			4		
			4		4

Mini Jigsaw

Fit the pieces in the grid to spell an outer garment in each row.

1					
2			A		
3		A			
4					
5		A			
6					

| O | R | | J | A | | A | N |
| A | Z | | P | O | | B | L |

| M | A | | N | T | | C | K |
| B | O | | L | E | | N | C |

| E | T | | A | K | | L | E |
| H | O | | E | R | | R | O |

Set Square

Place one each of the digits 1–9 in each grid to make the sums
work. Sums should be solved from left to right, or from top to bottom.

3	×		−		= 9
+		+		×	
	+		+		= 20
−		−		÷	
	×	1	÷		= 4

=	=	=
2	8	27

7	×		÷		= 14
−		÷		+	
	×		−		= 9
×		+		+	
	×	6	−		= 9

=	=	=
6	10	14

Pathfinder

Beginning with FROM RUSSIA WITH LOVE, and moving up, down, left, or right, trace a path through ten James Bond films.

```
L  L  I  V  E  A  N  D  T  D  I
L  O  R  O  C  O  S  L  E  M  E
I  Y  I  N  T  O  T  E  R  O  O
K  A  S  Y  S  P  H  K  A  R  N
A  L  A  C  S  U  G  Y  A  N  I
O  E  M  O  R  F  I  L  D  G  V
T  G  R  U  T  H  L  O  E  L  I
W  O  L  S  I  W  E  V  H  T  E
E  F  D  S  I  A  Y  L  Y  L  C
I  I  N  G  E  R  O  N  V  I  I
V  A  O  N  R  D  U  O  E  T  W
```

Number Jig

Place all of the listed numbers in the grid.

3 digits	5 digits	59543
272	29680	59667
474	29710	
577	37443	7 digits
674	39517	2463695
752	39547	2467625
759	47713	
~~954~~		
979		

4 digits
2645
2746
5036
5937
6047
6243
6245
6775
7236
7243
7292
7848

74

Fitword

Place all but one of the listed words in the grid. When the grid is complete, which word is left over?

3 letters	5 letters	6 letters
Act	Audio	Wailed
Bat	Corgi	Waited
Beg	Laden	
Due	Motto	
Eau	~~Older~~	
Gnu	Virgo	
Gum		
Hob		
Hum		
Mat		

4 letters

Agog
Avow
Dare
Hope
Host
Tome
Tuba
Went

Futoshiki

Fill the blank squares so that each row and column contains all the numbers 1, 2, and 3. Use the given numbers and the symbols to indicate if the number in the square is larger (>) or smaller (<) than the number next to it.

Jigsaw

Use the jigsaw pieces to re-create this completed crossword. Only the clues for the Across words have been given, but the pattern of the grid should help you as it is symmetrical from top right to bottom left.

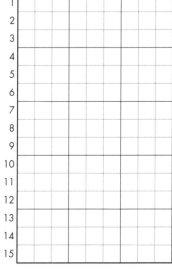

ACROSS

1 Newspapers and magazines
2 Vacuous, senseless
3 Once more
4 Malevolent ghost
5 Rear of a ship
6 Gumming, pasting
7 Strong desire

8 Almond, for example
9 Green-eyed monster
10 Declared
11 Increase

12 Pierce (with a needle)
13 Clumsy
14 Purify
15 Variety of piano

Totalized

Follow the instructions from top to bottom, starting with the number given to reach an answer at the foot of the ladder. Try to solve the problem in your head.

TOTALIZED

EASY	MEDIUM	HARD
14	28	6
DOUBLE IT	75% OF IT	CUBE IT
+ 12	+ 100	- 57
÷ 10	÷ 11	÷ 3
x 4	x 8	x 4
+ 17	+ ½ OF IT	+ 50% OF IT
÷ 3	- 32	- 6
x 6	÷ 5	÷ 6
- 29	x 7	+ 75% OF IT
DOUBLE IT	- 67	x 9
ANSWER	ANSWER	ANSWER

Initials

If **ITHOTN** (Oscar-winning film) is *In the Heat of the Night*, what do these initials represent?

1 **CM** (Chinese meal)

_____

2 **CBAH** (Proverb)

_____

3 **AYLT** (Elvis song)

_____

4 **IFAPIFAP** (Proverb)

_____

5 **TFC** (Gene Hackman film)

_____

Cell Block

Complete the grid by drawing blocks along the grid lines. Each block must contain the number of squares indicated by the digit inside it. Each block must contain only one digit and be a rectangle or square.

2		4			2
	1			1	2
		4			
3					5
	1			4	
2			5		

Mini Jigsaw

Fiit the pieces in the grid to spell a film term in each row.

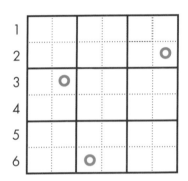

Set Square

Place one each of the digits 1–9 in each grid to make the sums work. Sums should be solved from left to right, or from top to bottom.

8	−		×		= 18
−		+		+	
	÷		+		= 11
×		÷		−	
	+	7	−		= 9

=		=		=
12		1		14

	+		−	3	= 12
−		+		+	
1	×		+		= 15
+		−		÷	
	×		÷		= 10

=		=		=
9		12		5

Pathfinder

Beginning with AVIONICS, and moving up, down, left, or right, one letter at a time, trace a path through twenty-one words associated with flying.

L	I	F	T	W	I	I	O	N	N	E
T	P	R	I	A	N	T	A	G	O	S
R	O	B	A	L	G	H	U	I	V	A
B	N	I	C	I	A	T	L	L	C	N
R	A	C	S	I	V	T	S	C	O	T
E	K	I	N	O	A	R	U	K	P	I
R	D	I	N	G	P	H	T	Y	R	U
U	N	I	F	T	I	R	U	A	B	T
D	A	N	A	O	L	E	N	W	U	N
D	L	R	I	R	O	C	N	E	L	A
E	R	W	A	Y	C	K	E	T	S	P

Number Jig

Place all of the listed numbers in the grid.

3 digits
325
371
436
572
576
~~632~~
~~836~~
672

4 digits
1027
2226
3195
3961
~~4607~~
~~4653~~
5023
5028
5403
6957
7681
9614

5 digits
26357
26464
26753
~~29025~~
76725
95058

95081
96082

7 digits
1234567
1535667

84

Fitword

Place all but one of the listed words in the grid. When the grid is complete, which word is left over?

3 letters
Cud
Ego
Emu
Gym
Hit
Jaw
Owe
Sow
Wax
Web

4 letters
Bomb
Defy
Limp
Luck
Nest
Pair
Sawn
Zany

5 letters
Annoy
Aorta
Aroma
Media
Merit
Minus

6 letters
Obtain
Rotund

Futoshiki

Fill the blank squares so that each row and column contains all the numbers 1, 2, and 3. Use the given numbers and the symbols to indicate if the number in the square is larger (>) or smaller (<) than the number next to it.

Jigsaw

Use the jigsaw pieces to re-create this completed crossword. Only the clues for the Across words have been given, but the pattern of the grid should help you as it is symmetrical from top right to bottom left.

ACROSS

1 Give away treacherously
2 Settee, couch
3 A rodent-catching dog
4 Not all
5 Medicinal quantity
6 Little mythical creature • Elapse

7 Feline
8 Cautious
9 Policeman
10 Strap of a bridle • Flow back

11 Nourish
12 Large spindle
13 Vexed, chagrined
14 Soil
15 Obey

Totalized

Follow the instructions from top to bottom, starting with the number given to reach an answer at the foot of the ladder. Try to solve the problem in your head.

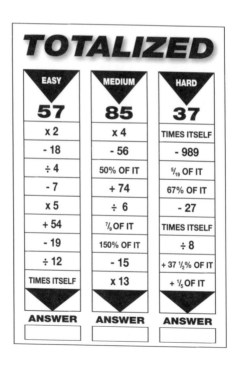

TOTALIZED

EASY	MEDIUM	HARD
57	**85**	**37**
x 2	x 4	TIMES ITSELF
- 18	- 56	- 989
÷ 4	50% OF IT	$^5/_{19}$ OF IT
- 7	+ 74	67% OF IT
x 5	÷ 6	- 27
+ 54	$^7/_9$ OF IT	TIMES ITSELF
- 19	150% OF IT	÷ 8
÷ 12	- 15	+ 37 ½% OF IT
TIMES ITSELF	x 13	+ $^1/_5$ OF IT
ANSWER	ANSWER	ANSWER

Initials

If **ITHOTN** (Oscar-winning film) is *In the Heat of the Night*, what do these initials represent?

1 **TAJ** (Cartoon duo)

Tom and Jerry

2 **FWTBT** (Classic novel)

For Whom the Bells Toll

3 **KOTG** (Park notice)

Keep off the Grass

4 **BAT** (Audrey Hepburn film)

Breakfast at T. Iffanys

5 **PGTW** (Nursery rhyme song)

Pop Goes the Weasel

Cell Block

Complete the grid by drawing blocks along the grid lines. Each block must contain the number of squares indicated by the digit inside it. Each block must contain only one digit and be a rectangle or square.

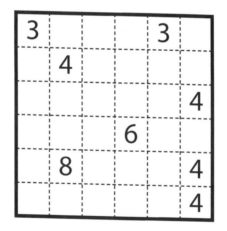

Mini Jigsaw

Fit the pieces in the grid to spell an African nation in each row.

1			
2	**A**		
3			
4		**A**	
5			
6			**A**

D A	U G	A N
I A	Z A	G A

L A	W I	A N
A N	D A	M B

L A	G O	M A
I A	M B	R W

Set Square

Place one each of the digits 1–9 in each grid to make the sums work. Sums should be solved from left to right, or from top to bottom.

	×		−		= 17
+		+		÷	
	+		÷	2	= 5
÷		+		+	
6	+		−		= 3

= 2   = 13   = 10

	×	5	−		= 12
+		+		×	
	+		÷		= 5
+		−		−	
	+		−	6	= 4

= 8   = 7   = 10

Pathfinder

Beginning LOAFING, and moving up, down, left, or right, one letter at a time, trace a path through sixteen words meaning "lazy."

G	D	D	P	K	L	S	L	C	R	A
N	I	O	L	C	A	X	A	I	G	H
O	R	K	S	H	O	R	O	U	S	T
W	A	C	I	Y	U	G	I	P	T	E
E	L	I	S	L	A	N	D	R	O	L
V	I	A	K	C	H	S	R	I	S	S
I	D	D	A	A	L	I	E	M	S	G
S	L	E	I	U	G	G	L	T	H	N
S	A	P	N	L	S	S	E	F	I	I
T	I	M	D	E	D	S	E	N	A	F
N	E	L	O	T	A	V	R	E	O	L

Number Jig

Place all of the listed numbers in the grid.

3 digits
261
350
351
851
855
861
956
999

4 digits
1049
1066
1943
2013
2382
3379
5062
5362
7016
7309
8394
9194

5 digits
11789
12784
21683
32019
32020
32589

41019
52584

7 digits
4825309
7626321

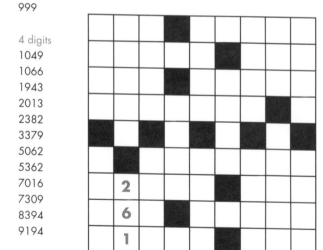

Fitword

Place all but one of the listed words in the grid. When the grid is complete, which word is left over?

3 letters	5 letters	6 letters
Boy	Admit	Legume
Fax	Flung	Resume
Gym	Mixer	
Mop	Pluck	
Oft	Prize	
~~Opt~~	Unify	
Orb		
Sty		
Yam		

4 letters
Espy
Ewer
Felt
Opal
Skim
Soft
Spar
Star
Sump

O P T

95

Futoshiki

Fill the blank squares so that each row and column contains all the numbers 1, 2, and 3. Use the given numbers and the symbols to indicate if the number in the square is larger (>) or smaller (<) than the number next to it.

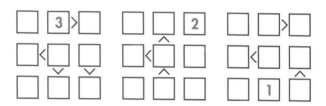

Jigsaw

Use the jigsaw pieces to re-create this completed crossword. Only the clues for the Across words have been given, but the pattern of the grid should help you as it is symmetrical from top right to bottom left.

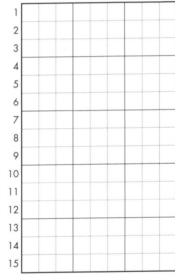

ACROSS

1 Doctor for animals
2 Passenger-carrying car • Leave out
3 Half a dozen
4 Chair, eg • Colored part of the eye
5 Boogie, bop
6 Sailors' drink • Small green vegetable
7 Bury
8 Measurement of land • Confidential assistant
9 Conscious
10 Half a barrel • Compete
11 Lax
12 Ship's team of workers • Prepare material for publication
13 Forthwith, immediately
14 On a former occasion • Wide-mouthed pitcher
15 Fisherman's long stick with a reel

97

Totalized

Follow the instructions from top to bottom, starting with the number given to reach an answer at the foot of the ladder. Try to solve the problem in your head.

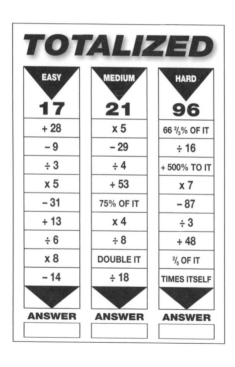

TOTALIZED

EASY	MEDIUM	HARD
17	**21**	**96**
+ 28	x 5	66 ⅔% OF IT
– 9	– 29	÷ 16
÷ 3	÷ 4	+ 500% TO IT
x 5	+ 53	x 7
– 31	75% OF IT	– 87
+ 13	x 4	÷ 3
÷ 6	÷ 8	+ 48
x 8	DOUBLE IT	⅖ OF IT
– 14	÷ 18	TIMES ITSELF
ANSWER	ANSWER	ANSWER

Initials

If **ITHOTN** (Oscar-winning film) is *In the Heat of the Night*, what do these initials represent?

1 **GC** (Discriminatory limit)

_____

2 **JTG** (Be too early)

_____

3 **SDML** (Reminisce)

_____

4 **DJAMH** (Horror story)

_____

5 **BYOH** (Brag)

_____

Cell Block

Complete the grid by drawing blocks along the grid lines. Each block must contain the number of squares indicated by the digit inside it. Each block must contain only one digit and be a rectangle or square.

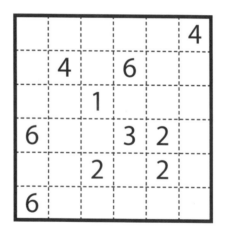

1

C	A	S	K	E	T
H	A	T	B	O	X
B	U	C	K	E	T
S	H	E	A	T	H
M	O	R	T	A	R
P	U	N	N	E	T

2

4	+	7	−	8
+		−		−
9	+	1	÷	5
−		×		×
2	+	3	+	6

2	×	8	+	3
+		×		×
1	+	9	−	4
×		÷		−
5	×	6	−	7

3

M	E	S	O	G	L	E	E	F	K	E
A	I	L	R	I	N	N	N	G	R	E
R	S	Y	E	L	G	E	R	U	F	T
Y	A	B	R	S	A	R	M	N	E	N
D	I	L	A	P	M	O	A	E	M	I
C	A	L	C	U	T	J	R	M	T	R
I	K	I	A	R	M	E	R	Y	H	E
N	N	R	R	D	E	G	I	C	O	D
M	A	P	A	A	M	A	N	A	R	N
O	A	R	P	M	O	S	O	G	E	A
N	T	R	A	G	O	N	C	O	R	I

Turmeric, Oregano, Coriander,
Thyme, Mint, Fenugreek,
Fennel, Ginger, Marjoram,
Parsley, Basil, Rosemary,
Dill, Cardamom, Paprika,
Cinnamon, Tarragon, Sage

4

7		4	1	4	5	3		9
7	5	5	3		3	4	5	0
6	6	0	2		2	8	6	1
8	5	9		3	9	9	7	2
	4		5	5	5		6	
3	5	9	7	7		1	7	9
8	6	2	4		8	8	6	8
4	5	1	0		3	0	5	4
4		4	9	0	3	5		9

Leftover number: 7786

5

F	U	M	E		S	L	U	M
O		O		A	I		I	A
W	I	T		G	I	V	E	R
L		T		O		I		T
	C	O	L		I	D	L	Y
M		I	L	L				R
O	N	C	E		K	I	N	
A		H		A		M		F
N	E	A	R	S		A	C	E
E		R		P		G		L
R	U	M	P		G	O	A	L

Leftover word: GLUT

6

1	3	2		1	3	2		2	1	3
2	1	3		3	2	1		1	3	2
3	2	1		2	1	3		3	2	1

7

M		T	A	R	I	F	F
O	W	E		A		E	G
R		L	I	T	E	R	A	L
A	L	L		M		A	
S			F	I	E	N	D
S	K	I		E		N	D
		R	E	A	C	T	
T	O	R		S		I	O	N
A		E	A	T	E	N	
N		L		E		G	U	M
K	N	E	A	D			E
A		V			A	R	M
R	E	A	R	I	N	G	O
D		N	L		E	R	R	Y
	S	T	Y	L	E	D	Y

8

EASY:	84
MEDIUM:	24
HARD:	129

9 1 Samson and Delilah

2 *Raiders of the Lost Ark*

3 *To Kill a Mockingbird*

4 The Golden Gate Bridge

5 *Pride and Prejudice*

10

4				3	
					3
			6		
	6	4			2
		1			
3				4	

11

F	O	D	D	E	R
C	A	T	T	L	E
S	L	U	R	R	Y
M	A	N	U	R	E
F	A	L	L	O	W
S	I	L	A	G	E

12

3	+	9	−	5
×		+		×
7	+	1	÷	4
−		−		÷
6	+	8	÷	2

6	×	8	÷	3
×		÷		×
4	+	1	×	2
−		−		+
9	+	7	−	5

solutions

13

F	O	O	C	P	R	E	N	D	W	H
R	P	D	I	L	S	S	A	E	R	I
O	S	S	A	R	C	O	L	E	C	S
C	E	O	G	L	N	A	C	P	U	K
L	L	R	O	W	O	P	N	A	A	S
E	A	M	B	G	N	E	L	E	N	D
T	N	M	I	N	E	R	B	I	Y	E
S	I	T	X	I	D	A	G	N	R	R
P	A	E	C	E	L	L	P	R	F	S
U	T	K	A	R	M	N	A	E	E	I
L	A	T	H	E	O	M	E	T	V	E

Food processor, Mallet, Spatula, Thermometer, Frying pan, Ladle, Cake tin, Mixing bowl, Garlic press, Colander, Whisk, Saucepan, Can opener, Blender, Sieve

14

4		6	1	0	2	9		8
1	5	2	5		3	4	5	6
8	7	6	0		4	8	9	2
4	5	9		4	5	0	5	0
	8		3	7	6		8	
6	5	7	3	9		4	5	6
8	9	2	4		4	1	7	5
3	5	9	5		7	6	5	4
0		4	6	0	0	2		0

Leftover number: 6479

15

L	O	B	E		A	B	L	E
O		I		A		L		N
F	I	N		W	H	I	Z	Z
T		G		E		N		Y
	S	O	W		S	K	I	M
A		E	A	U				E
S	N	U	B		P	L	Y	
T		P		F		E		G
H	A	S	T	E		A	I	R
M		E		W		N		A
A	N	T	E		S	T	A	B

Leftover word: SIP

16

1	2	3		3	2	1		1	2	3
3	1	2		1	3	2		2	3	1
2	3	1		2	1	3		3	1	2

17

18 EASY: 71

MEDIUM: 43

HARD: 161

19 1 "Hickory Dickory Dock"

2 *The War of the Worlds*

3 *Pirates of the Caribbean*

4 Great Barrier Reef

5 One good turn deserves another

20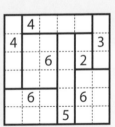

21

C	O	T	T	O	N
T	H	R	E	A	D
L	I	N	I	N	G
F	A	B	R	I	C
N	E	E	D	L	E
S	T	I	T	C	H

22

3	×	6	+	2
×		+		×
7	+	4	−	1
−		÷		+
9	+	5	−	8

7	+	8	÷	5
×		+		+
4	+	1	−	3
−		+		+
9	+	6	−	2

23

E	R	G	A	N	I	M	U	G	R	E
T	E	M	B	E	L	P	H	O	O	H
P	L	U	H	T	Y	T	L	E	S	T
E	W	W	T	E	D	S	E	U	M	O
T	O	H	I	M	U	N	T	H	B	M
E	N	S	S	P	H	A	M	S	U	P
R	P	I	G	T	Y	T	O	S	I	S
N	A	P	E	L	T	S	T	B	N	K
R	A	P	T	T	H	R	O	O	O	C
Z	N	U	I	L	E	E	N	G	L	I
E	L	A	L	A	D	D	I	O	L	D

Hansel, Humpty Dumpty,
Three Little Pigs, Snow White,
Thumbelina, Gretel, Peter Pan,
Rapunzel, Aladdin, Goldilocks,
Puss in Boots, Tom Thumb,
Mother Goose

24

2		3	3	4	5	5		7
5	7	2	6		9	6	7	1
7	6	7	7		6	7	4	3
3	5	4		5	7	8	5	9
	3		3	6	4		3	
7	4	7	5	4		5	6	7
9	2	4	4		5	6	2	4
5	1	7	8		2	2	1	5
8		7	2	6	7	9		9

Leftover number: 5241

solutions

25

M	A	K	E		T	S	A	R
U		H		E		U		H
S	P	A		B	U	L	K	Y
K		K		B		K		M
	B	I	B		B	Y	T	E
A		O	N	E			S	
A	S	W	I	G		D	E	N
S		C		E		A		A
U	N	I	T	Y		R	I	G
R		N		E		L		E
E	D	G	Y		D	Y	E	D

Leftover word: HOLY

26

1	3	2		3	1	2		1	2	3
2	1	3		2	3	1		3	1	2
3	2	1		1	2	3		2	3	1

27

28 EASY: 64

MEDIUM: 20

HARD: 27

29
1. "Deck the Halls"
2. *My Fair Lady*
3. *Gone with the Wind*
4. *The Bridge Over the River Kwai*
5. The Jackson Five

30

	3			3	
		5			
	4				5
			3		
	3				
4				4	2

31

C	O	L	U	M	N
E	R	R	A	T	A
M	A	R	G	I	N
L	E	T	T	E	R
F	O	R	M	A	T
O	F	F	S	E	T

32

2	×	4	−	1
×		×		+
7	−	6	+	9
−		÷		−
5	+	8	−	3

6	÷	3	+	9
+		×		−
8	+	4	−	7
÷		−		+
2	÷	1	×	5

33

U	T	I	N	E	S	T	A	M	O	P
O	R	E	V	U	T	R	T	E	S	D
M	P	R	O	R	C	U	S	T	I	L
I	Y	R	C	E	C	T	E	R	H	C
I	T	A	N	I	H	I	O	N	V	E
L	T	A	E	N	G	T	B	P	I	T
I	H	H	T	I	H	A	R	O	S	I
B	A	C	I	B	A	T	E	S	O	P
I	C	S	O	A	M	I	A	E	S	X
X	O	N	U	G	E	D	T	H	R	A
E	L	F	S	O	Y	G	N	I	E	L

Breathing, Yoga, Meditation, Poses, Relax, Positive, Child pose, Mat, Stretching, Habit, Hatha, Conscious, Flexibility, Improve, Routine, Structure, Crane

34

2		2	3	4	3	4		2
5	4	8	1		5	3	4	8
3	4	0	8		1	7	4	0
2	4	0		3	6	1	5	2
	5		2	1	2		5	
5	6	1	5	3		4	5	9
3	6	1	1		4	6	6	6
4	6	5	6		5	1	6	0
1		4	3	4	3	4		0

Leftover number: 2552

35

F	O	N	D		T	S	A	R
L		Y		A		O		A
O	I	L		F	L	O	W	N
G		O		T		T		K
	A	N	D		P	Y	R	E
S		U	S	E				D
M	I	N	E		T	H	Y	
O		A		D		E		G
K	I	T	T	Y		A	D	O
E		T		E		D		S
D	A	Y	S		M	Y	T	H

Leftover word: MIRE

36

2	3	1		3	1	2		2	3	1
3	1	2		2	3	1		3	1	2
1	2	3		1	2	3		1	2	3

37

38 EASY: 29
MEDIUM: 144
HARD: 115

39 1 The Battle of Hastings

2 The Hanging Gardens
of Babylon

3 *Mona Lisa*

4 *Seven Brides for Seven
Brothers*

5 Hercule Poirot

40

3				2	
			8		
2					
5					6
				5	
	3		2		

41

R	E	C	I	P	E
P	I	C	N	I	C
C	O	U	R	S	E
R	A	T	I	O	N
S	I	M	M	E	R
B	U	F	F	E	T

42

5	×	6	÷	2
+		×		×
9	+	1	−	8
−		×		÷
7	−	3	×	4

2	×	3	+	4
×		×		+
5	×	6	−	7
−		÷		÷
8	+	9	−	1

43

```
M P R G C R I E T E R
R Y A U L S C K B T F
O I N G M E D E U T L
W S S I A I L P F L Y
U G L T N M L I E E W
B C O C U L I D G A A
Y E N T S E V I M P S
D A T S P E W L I A N
A L I P I D E R F R S
D I C E D E G R I U Y
A C Y L F N E E T F L
```

Centipede, Greenfly, Cicada, Ladybugs, Worm, Praying mantis, Locust, Spider, Fruit fly, Snail, Weevil, Millipede, Slug, Cricket, Butterfly, Wasp, Midge, Flea

44

5		4	4	0	7	9		2
4	1	5	0		6	1	5	0
2	8	2	8		6	8	2	8
8	5	9		3	7	6	6	8
	2		4	1	2		4	
3	6	6	2	8		3	7	4
2	4	8	2		3	4	8	2
6	7	1	0		6	7	1	5
5		9	7	4	0	8		9

Leftover number: 5172

111

45

```
R A T E   A M I D
A   R   O   O   U
C O O   P A N E L
Y   L   T   E   C
  A L L   T Y P E
D   E G O       T
A B U T   T A T
H   N   O   R   E
L A C E D   R I D
I   U   D   A   E
A R T Y   H Y M N
```

Leftover word: RIOT

46

```
3 2 1   3 1 2   3 2 1
1 3 2   2 3 1   1 3 2
2 1 3   1 2 3   2 1 3
```

47

```
  U   C   S   B
B L U R   H O U R
  N   E G O   R
P A C E   R U N G
R   O L D E N   O
I O N   U   D I D
N   G O O S E   P
C R E W   A R I A
I   S L O P S   R
P O T   R   I R E
A   E B B E D   N
L O D E   L E N T
E   R I C E   O
A G O G   C O R N
  Y   E   T   M
```

48 EASY: 72

MEDIUM: 361

HARD: 185

49
1 A watched pot never boils

2 Spaghetti Bolognese

3 *The Owl and the Pussycat*

4 *The Witches of Eastwick*

5 "My Heart Will Go On"

50

	4			2		
3			4			3
				3		
3		2				
	3		4			
		5				

51

R	A	D	I	U	M
N	I	C	K	E	L
C	A	R	B	O	N
C	O	P	P	E	R
S	I	L	V	E	R
H	E	L	I	U	M

52

9	−	2	×	3
+		+		+
7	+	6	−	8
−		÷		−
1	+	4	÷	5

6	÷	2	+	8
−		×		+
3	×	9	−	7
×		−		−
5	×	4	+	1

53

V	A	O	S	W	H	I	H	A	L	P
E	L	N	M	T	N	T	E	Z	E	U
N	C	R	I	A	E	M	E	N	I	R
D	E	U	L	B	G	A	R	A	R	P
E	R	I	O	I	N	E	T	M	A	L
M	A	L	N	R	A	U	L	U	R	E
B	E	I	O	C	M	A	U	S	H	A
T	R	M	R	H	D	A	Q	S	K	K
U	E	V	E	R	L	O	G	E	T	I
R	S	I	S	E	L	E	N	D	I	V
Q	U	O	C	A	R	T	A	I	R	I

White, Hazel, Purple, Russet, Khaki, Viridian, Gold, Aquamarine, Ultramarine, Magenta, Blue, Crimson, Lavender, Amber, Turquoise, Vermilion, Ochre, Scarlet

54

2	6	2	■	7	7	1	2	7
9	3	0	6	3	■	5	0	6
6	5	4	■	1	3	0	0	4
8	2	8	3	8	4	8	■	5
■	0	■	4	■	2	■	2	■
1	■	8	2	8	3	8	4	9
6	9	7	0	3	■	5	6	0
2	5	0	■	1	6	3	0	9
2	3	5	2	8	■	6	7	4

55

C	U	S	P		S	L	I	P
O		P		O	O		A	
W	H	O		N	E	W	E	R
L		O		E	E		T	
	O	F	F		T	R	U	E
P		A	G	O			D	
H	O	A	X		G	A	P	
O		W		G		B		H
N	I	F	T	Y		A	R	E
E		U		M		C		M
D	O	L	E		S	K	E	P

Leftover word: FEN

56

2	1	3
3	2	1
1	3	2

2	3	1
3	1	2
1	2	3

3	1	2
2	3	1
1	2	3

57

```
  F TOUR
ALTO N F
 O TASSEL
PUPA O R
 T L PORT
  SIGH Y
 COT I M
TUNA SCAT
S R TON
T IRIS
ROTA C E
 M N ARMY
SEXIST B
 R S EWER
  AMID D
```

58

EASY:	43
MEDIUM:	67
HARD:	99

59

1 Peach Melba

2 *Butch Cassidy and the Sundance Kid*

3 Acorn squash

4 Sistine Chapel

5 Vincent Van Gogh

60

```
 8      |
--------+----
   3 1  | 6
--------+----
     3  |
 6      | 3 2
--------+----
   4    |
```

61

G	A	N	N	E	T
O	S	P	R	E	Y
G	R	O	U	S	E
O	R	I	O	L	E
C	U	C	K	O	O
P	L	O	V	E	R

62

9	–	3	×	2
+		×		×
1	×	4	+	6
÷		–		÷
5	+	7	–	8

9	+	6	–	5
–		×		+
7	–	4	+	1
×		÷		÷
3	×	8	÷	2

63

E	D	L	E	C	I	T	I	V	H	A
U	E	K	I	U	O	N	A	E	L	I
T	Z	E	B	S	J	J	H	R	E	M
E	R	J	O	A	H	O	S	E	J	H
N	O	L	A	B	A	U	H	M	I	A
O	I	E	K	K	J	G	E	S	C	I
M	N	E	K	U	U	D	M	E	A	D
Y	A	X	O	A	H	L	A	N	H	A
N	D	H	D	I	N	A	H	T	O	B
A	H	A	U	S	Z	E	P	A	T	I
M	U	I	M	E	H	E	N	S	N	O

Judges, Micah, Obadiah,
Jeremiah, Leviticus, Jonah,
Joshua, Habakkuk, Exodus,
Zephaniah, Lamentations,
Nehemiah, Daniel, Job, Ezekiel,
Deuteronomy, Nahum

64

4	6	2	■	6	7	4	3	6
5	7	2	3	1	■	5	4	1
8	0	0	■	7	5	2	5	1
1	3	4	5	6	7	8	■	5
■	2	■	7	■	3	■	6	■
8	■	2	3	4	5	6	7	8
7	5	0	8	2	■	7	2	7
3	4	2	■	7	4	1	3	1
5	5	4	3	1	■	6	6	4

solutions

· ·

65

D	Y	E	R		P	A	I	R
U		N		B		I	E	
P	I	N		A	P	R	I	L
E		U		Y		Y	E	I
	R	I	B		A	D	Z	E
H			I	M	P			F
O	P	E	N		T	A	T	
L		R	S		R		R	A
I	N	E	R	T		R	I	G
E		C		Y		A		E
R	O	T	E		E	Y	E	D

Leftover word: GAME

66

3	2	1		2	1	3		2	1	3
1	3	2		1	3	2		3	2	1
2	1	3		3	2	1		1	3	2

67

D	A	U	B		B	O	W	L
E		O	D	E			I	
C		B	O	U	G	H		N
A	G	O		T		I	C	E
M		A	B	Y	S	S		A
P	U	R	R		U	S	E	R
	N		I	L	L		M	
O	D	D	S		T	U	B	E
	U		T	E	A		E	
P	E	A	L		N	O	D	E
E		R	E	C	A	P		R
R	I	M		L		E	R	A
I		Y	E	A	R	N		S
O		A	N	Y			E	
D	I	E	T		E	M	I	R

68 EASY: 121
    MEDIUM: 154
    HARD: 7

69
1 King Kong
2 David and Goliath
3 The Leaning Tower of Pisa
4 Foot and mouth disease
5 Simon and Garfunkel

70

1		5			
	4		2	2	
				2	2
6			4		
			4		4

71

A	N	O	R	A	K
B	L	A	Z	E	R
J	A	C	K	E	T
P	O	N	C	H	O
M	A	N	T	L	E
B	O	L	E	R	O

72

3	×	5	–	6
+		+		×
7	+	4	+	9
–		–		÷
8	×	1	÷	2

7	×	8	÷	4
–		÷		+
5	×	2	–	1
×		+		+
3	×	6	–	9

73

```
L L I V E A N D T D I
L O R O C O S L E M E
I Y I N T O T E R O O
K A S Y S P H K A R N
A L A C S U G Y A N I
O E M O R F I L D G V
T G R U T H L O E L I
W O L S I W E V H T E
E F D S I A Y L Y L C
I I N G E R O N V I I
V A O N R D U O E T W
```

From Russia with Love, You Only Live Twice, The Living Daylights, Octopussy, Casino Royale, Goldfinger, Dr. No, A View to a Kill, Live and Let Die, Moonraker

74

7	5	2		5	9	6	6	7
2	9	7	1	0		2	7	2
9	5	4		3	7	4	4	3
2	4	6	7	6	2	5		6
	3		8		4		3	
6		2	4	6	3	6	9	5
2	9	6	8	0		7	5	9
4	7	4		4	7	7	1	3
3	9	5	4	7		5	7	7

75

```
T O M E   A V O W
U   O   A   I   A
B A T   C O R G I
A   T   T   G   T
  H O B   H O P E
W   E A U       D
A G O G   M A T
I   L   G   U   W
L A D E N   D U E
E   E U   I   N
D A R E   H O S T
```

Leftover word: GUM

76

```
2 1 3   2 3 1   2 3 1
1 3 2   3 1 2   3 1 2
3 2 1   1 2 3   1 2 3
```

77

78 EASY: 74

MEDIUM: 73

HARD: 819

79
1 Chow mein

2 Charity begins at home

3 "Are You Lonesome Tonight?"

4 In for a penny, in for a pound

5 *The French Connection*

80

2		4			2
	1			1	2
		4			
3					5
	1			4	
2			5		

81

W	E	E	P	I	E
S	T	U	D	I	O
C	O	M	E	D	Y
S	E	Q	U	E	L
C	A	M	E	R	A
B	I	O	P	I	C

82

8	−	5	×	6
−		+		+
4	÷	2	+	9
×		÷		−
3	+	7	−	1

6	+	9	−	3
−		+		+
1	×	8	+	7
+		−		÷
4	×	5	÷	2

83

L	I	F	T	W	I	I	O	N	N	E
T	P	R	I	A	N	T	A	G	O	S
R	O	B	A	L	G	H	U	I	V	A
B	N	I	C	I	A	T	L	L	C	N
R	A	C	S	I	V	T	S	C	O	T
E	K	I	N	O	A	R	U	K	P	I
R	D	I	N	G	P	H	T	Y	R	U
U	N	I	F	T	I	R	U	A	B	T
D	A	N	A	O	L	E	N	W	U	N
D	L	R	I	R	O	C	N	E	L	A
E	R	W	A	Y	C	K	E	T	S	P

Avionics, Cabin, Brake, Rudder,
Landing, Pilot, Fin, Airway,
Rocket, Span, Turbulence,
Runway, Thrust, Tail, Airport,
Lift, Wing, Hull, Cockpit,
Navigation, Nose

84

3	2	5		2	6	4	6	4
9	6	0	8	2		6	3	6
6	7	2		2	9	0	2	5
1	5	3	5	6	6	7		3
	3		0		1		2	
6		1	2	3	4	5	6	7
9	5	0	8	1		4	3	6
5	7	2		9	5	0	5	8
7	6	7	2	5		3	7	1

85

L	I	M	P		P	A	I	R
U		E		E		O		O
C	U	D		M	E	R	I	T
K		I		U		T		U
	J	A	W		S	A	W	N
O			E	G	O			D
B	O	M	B		W	A	X	
T		I		G		R		D
A	N	N	O	Y		O	W	E
I		U		M		M		F
N	E	S	T		Z	A	N	Y

Leftover word: HIT

86

2	3	1		3	1	2		1	3	2
1	2	3		1	2	3		3	2	1
3	1	2		2	3	1		2	1	3

87

88

EASY:	100
MEDIUM:	351
HARD:	330

122

89
1. Tom and Jerry
2. *For Whom the Bell Tolls*
3. Keep off the grass
4. *Breakfast at Tiffany's*
5. "Pop Goes the Weasel"

90

3			3	
	4			
				4
		6		
	8			4
				4

91

A	N	G	O	L	A
G	A	M	B	I	A
M	A	L	A	W	I
R	W	A	N	D	A
U	G	A	N	D	A
Z	A	M	B	I	A

92

3	×	7	–	4
+		+		÷
9	+	1	÷	2
÷		+		+
6	+	5	–	8

4	×	5	–	8
+		+		×
1	+	9	÷	2
+		–		–
3	+	7	–	6

93

```
G D D P K L S L C R A
N I O L C A X A I G H
O R K S H O R O U S T
W A C I Y U G I P T E
E L I S L A N D R O L
V I A K C H S R I S S
I D D A A L I E M S G
S L E I U G G L T H N
S A P N L S S E F I I
T I M D E D S E N A F
N E L O T A V R E O L
```

Loafing, Shiftless, Enervated,
Sluggish, Lackadaisical, Idle,
Indolent, Impassive, Workshy,
Languorous, Torpid, Remiss,
Lethargic, Lax, Slack, Plodding

94

8	5	5	■	1	1	7	8	9
3	2	0	1	9	■	3	5	1
9	5	6	■	4	1	0	1	9
4	8	2	5	3	0	9	■	4
■	4	■	3	■	6	■	3	■
1	■	7	6	2	6	3	2	1
3	2	0	2	0	■	3	5	0
8	6	1	■	1	2	7	8	4
2	1	6	8	3	■	9	9	9

95

```
S U M P . O P A L
O . I . O . L . E
F A X . F L U N G
T . E . T . C . U
. O R B . S K I M
R . O . P . T . E
E S P Y . Y A M
S . R . G . D . S
U N I F Y . M O P
M . Z . M . I . A
E W E R . S T A R
```

Leftover word: FELT

96

2 3 1	3 1 2	3 2 1
1 2 3	1 2 3	1 3 2
3 1 2	2 3 1	2 1 3

97

98 EASY: 42
MEDIUM: 3
HARD: 900

99
1 Glass ceiling

2 Jump the gun

3 Stroll down memory lane

4 *Dr. Jekyll and Mr. Hyde*

5 Blow your own horn

100

FREE PUZZLE SOCIETY MEMBERSHIP—

ACCESS TO THOUSANDS OF PUZZLES!

The Puzzle Society would like to thank you for your purchase by offering a free 90-day subscription to our online puzzle club. With this membership, you will have exclusive, unlimited access to 70+ updated puzzles added each week and 8,000+ archived puzzles.

To take advantage of this special membership offer, visit **Puzzlesociety.com/play/posh** and start playing today!

The Puzzle Society™
puzzlesociety.com

washingtonpost.com
Sunday Crossword